BOUNDARIES
A Guide For Teens

Also from the Boys Town Press

Show Me your Mad Face

Great Days Ahead

Competing with Character

Fathers, Come Home, 2nd Edition

There Are No Simple Rules for Dating My Daughter

Common Sense Parenting, 3rd Edition

Common Sense Parenting of Toddlers and Preschoolers

Practical Tools for Foster Parents

Take Two: Skill-Building Skits You Have Time to Do!

Teaching Social Skills to Youth

No Room for Bullies: Lesson Plans for Grades 5-8

No Room for Bullies: Lesson Plans for Grades 9-12

No Room for Bullies

For Adolescents

Friend Me! 10 Awesome Steps to Fun and Friendship

Dating! 10 Helpful Tips for a Successful Relationship

A Good Friend

What's Right for Me?

Guys, Lets Keep It Real!

Little Sisters, Listen Up!

For a free Boys Town Press catalog, call 1-800-282-6657

Visit our website at BoysTownPress.org

BOUNDARIES
A Guide For Teens

Val J. Peter & Tom Dowd

BOYS TOWN.
Press

Boys Town, Nebraska

Boundaries: A Guide for Teens

Published by The Boys Town Press
Father Flanagan's Boys' Home
Boys Town, NE 68010

ISBN-13: 978-1-889322-90-2
ISBN-10: 1-889322-90-3

Boys Town Press is the publishing division of Boys Town, a national organization serving children and families.

10 9 8 7 6 5

BOYS TOWN NATIONAL HOTLINE®
1-800-448-3000
A crisis, resource and referral number for kids and parents

Contents

BOUNDARIES

What Are Boundaries?

A boundary is the personal space that you keep between yourself and others. It defines "where I end and you begin." Boundaries work in two ways: They allow things in, and they keep things out. Boundaries are important because they define areas of privacy.

Good boundaries help you feel secure and worthwhile. When someone crosses the boundaries you have set, your mind and body tell you that the person has gone too far, and you start to feel uncomfortable.

Initially, parents help you begin setting your boundaries. Later, you take a more active role in setting your boundaries.

Types of Boundaries

Physical/Sexual – These boundaries protect your body. You decide who can touch you, how they can touch you, and where. These boundaries help you answer questions such as "Do I shake hands or give a hug?" Physical boundaries also protect private areas of the body.

Emotional/Spiritual – These boundaries protect your private thoughts and emotions. You decide what feelings you will or will not share with others. You share secret thoughts and some of your deepest feelings only with certain family members and friends.

Teresa's Story

Teresa always worried about how other people felt. She had been a "people pleaser" since she was a little girl. Now that she was older, she often thought of becoming a nurse.

Teresa first met Sam in the guidance counselor's office. She was switching classes to acquire a study hall at the end of the day. His family had just moved from New York, and he and the counselor were arranging his class schedule. Teresa and Sam finished working on their schedules at the same time. She asked him what he thought of the town and if he had any brothers and sisters, and they made the usual small talk for about five minutes.

As it turned out, they were in two of the same classes. Sam was talkative and asked questions all the time. They started eating lunch and studying for tests together. He talked about what it was like growing up in New York City, about his screwed-up family and the times he saw his dad beat his mom. These things disturbed Teresa, and she felt so sorry for him that she almost cried.

After the first few weeks of school, Sam started passing notes to Teresa after class. Soon the notes started to bother Teresa. They were too personal, and she noticed that Sam was becoming a little too friendly when they were talking. She had made it very clear that friendship was the only thing on her mind and that she didn't want to date Sam. But that didn't stop Sam from continually asking personal questions: What did she wear to bed – a nightgown or pajamas? What did she think was sexy about the guys she knew? What kinds of things "turned her on"?

Teresa was in a bind. She didn't want to hurt Sam's feelings because she knew he was really sensitive. But she hated those questions, and they made her uncomfortable. She tried to tell Sam in a nice way to stop it, but he just didn't get the hint. She finally decided that she had to tell him to quit asking her such personal questions.

The next day when they were eating lunch together, Sam began asking questions again. Teresa thought this was the perfect time to tell him what she was feeling. She said, "You know Sam, we've done a lot of stuff together..." He interrupted her: "You're gonna dump me, aren't you?" He had a hurt look on his face that upset her. She took a deep breath and said, "Well, no, not really. I just thought that some of the things you've been talking about lately have made me kind of uncomfortable."

Whew. She had said it. Teresa had always had trouble saying anything that she thought might hurt someone. She usually hedged instead of telling someone the straight truth. Sam wrinkled his face quizzically and said, "Like what?" Teresa told him that she didn't like talking about personal and private things, and then she gave him some examples. She said she didn't like being asked questions about sex, what she wore to bed and things like that.

He answered, "You know you like it, Teresa. I will give you whatever you want. You need me. Trust me. It will be fun."

Teresa was shocked. She realized that she should have been up front with Sam from the beginning. She realized that she needed to work on setting limits and letting people know exactly what those limits were. And it was clear that Sam knew exactly what he was doing. He had grown up in a dysfunctional family where such language was the way a man controlled a woman. Embarrassing a girl gave him a sense of power. His dad did it to his mom all the time.

Teresa and Sam broke up that day. And Teresa is happy they did. It was hard, but Teresa feels proud that she stood up for herself. She also gained respect from her classmates.

You Can Say 'Stop'

If you recognized that Sam was saying things that offended or embarrassed Teresa, good for you. You have an accurate picture of what personal boundaries are. You know Sam's own boundaries were full of holes, so full that he was overwhelming Teresa. And if you knew that Teresa should have said something earlier, you understand how important it is to let people know what your boundaries are.

It's not impolite or unreasonable to say "stop" whenever someone makes you feel uncomfortable or tries to make you do something that is wrong. It is important to realize that someone else's boundary violations are not your fault. If a violator will not stop, tell someone who can help you. Keep telling until the problem is taken care of.

When aggressive people don't have clear boundaries, they end up hurting others. When someone crosses a boundary line you have set, you should be uneasy. Think of your own experiences. Has a stranger ever stood so close to you that you were nervous? Has anyone ever touched you in a way that was "overly friendly"? Did someone you didn't know very well ever sneak up behind you and pinch or grab you or start rubbing your shoulders? Has anyone ever asked you personal questions that embarrassed or upset you?

Those are all boundary issues. Those people were just "too close for comfort."

What would you do if you were in Teresa's situation?

Your Boundary Wheel

It's important for people to know what you stand for. Your foundational values are the things that are really valuable and worthwhile to you in your heart of hearts and in your family. They are values that define your character, such as trustworthiness, respect, responsibility, fairness, caring, and citizenship.

To better understand your boundaries, imagine a series of circles forming a wheel around you. These circles can help you picture how close you will let someone get to you physically and how much emotional sharing you will do with this person.

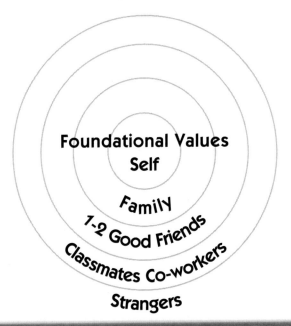

Foundational Values
Self
Family
1-2 Good Friends
Classmates Co-workers
Strangers

Everyone you encounter fits somewhere along your boundary wheel. Family and good friends are within the innermost circles. Casual acquaintances, classmates and co-workers are farther out, while strangers are the farthest away from you.

Where do the various people in your life fit within your boundary wheel? Write their names in the appropriate circles.

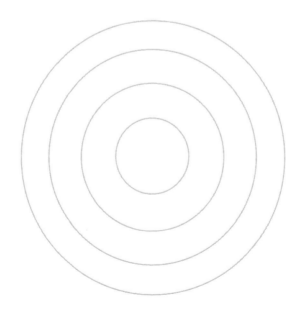

Healthy
BOUNDARIES

Bo's Story

Bo was a 16-year-old student from an all-boys school. He had met Mariah, a friend of his sister's, at a soccer game. There had been some romantic attraction between them the first time they met. Bo asked her out on a date, and she accepted. They talked, shared, and had a good time.

The talking was more satisfying than he could have ever imagined. She listened to what he had to say, and he did the same with her. They shared a few of their hopes and dreams with each other, both being encouraging and attentive. It was a new experience for Bo, and he enjoyed it greatly. It wasn't a lot, but it was a good start.

Bo and Mariah dated for a couple of months. Some of his close friends did a lot of teasing. They didn't understand about being friends with a girl and not trying to have sex, especially after a couple of months.

Bo felt very lucky to have a friend like Mariah. He ended up telling the guys who pressured him about the sex issue that it was none of their business.

Respecting Boundaries

Bo liked his boundaries and respected Mariah's boundaries as well. These two were becoming real friends, and they shared a lot of feelings. Many times the pressure to be "cool" pushes young men to hide their need for connected relationships, and they substitute sex for real friendship. They become demanding and even become "sexual con artists."

Bo and Mariah both felt good in their relationship, and it helped build their respect for the opposite sex. They began to see that the purpose of a boy-girl relationship at their age is friendship that is healthy, fun, and respectful of boundaries.

Guidelines for Healthy Boundaries

1. **How much you allow people within your physical and emotional boundaries usually depends on how long you've known them and how much you like and trust them.**

   What information you share with them depends on what your relationship is:

   - co-workers – not much information except social.

   - schoolmates – a bit of private information and lots of social information.

   - friends – lots of information, both private and social.

2. **The amount of self-disclosure should be based on how well you know others and how much you can trust them in appropriate ways.**

3. **You need to have reciprocal trust that is appropriate.**

   If your "friend" is not worthy of trust, he or she should not be in your inner circle.

4. **If you expect others to respect your boundaries, you must respect theirs.**

   If you are not worthy of trust, you should not be in their inner circles.

5. **When someone tries to violate your boundaries, use that experience to decide how you can handle similar situations in the future.**

6. **Trust your feelings of comfort and discomfort when you are around others.**

   If someone makes you uncomfortable, your boundary "radar" should go on alert.

7. **Never hesitate to ask a trusted adult questions about your boundaries and whether they are appropriate.**

   Remember that if you have been abused, your boundary "radar" can get mixed up. You may be used to ignoring feelings of discomfort, which in turn can prevent you from realizing immediately when someone violates your boundaries. It is important to talk with someone you can trust when you begin to wonder if something is right or wrong. Over time this can also help you get your own "radar" back on track.

8. Speak up when someone or something bothers you.

Let people know what you won't tolerate. Don't be afraid to say "no" to anyone who may be trying to hurt or take advantage of you.

Healthy boundaries help you to:

- Develop good healthy relationships, especially friendships.

- Enjoy true friends and family.

- Respect others and avoid arguing when they say "no" to you.

- Say "no" to someone else.

- Have a strong sense of self-respect.

- Share appropriate information with others.

- Expect shared responsibility for relationships.

- Recognize when a problem is yours and when it is someone else's.

- Not tolerate disrespect or abuse.

Persons with healthy boundaries:

- Are secure with themselves.

- Don't let others intrude on them.

- Have a clear sense of their own views, values, and priorities.

- Are able to identify safe and appropriate people.

- Are confident.

- Can protect themselves without shutting themselves off from others.

- Know how to stand up for themselves at appropriate times.

- Are able to enter into relationships with others without losing their identities.

- Don't reveal too much or too little.

What characteristics of healthy
boundaries do you have?

Can you think of other signs of
healthy boundaries that aren't on
the list?

An example of how a friend
respected my physical boundaries:

An example of how a friend
disrespected my physical boundaries:

An example of how a friend
respected my emotional boundaries:

An example of how a friend
disrespected my emotional
boundaries:

Have you ever felt your "radar" go on alert when someone made you feel uncomfortable? What was the situation?

How did you handle it?

Boundaries Protect

Healthy boundaries protect a person's body, thoughts, and feelings. On the other hand, unhealthy boundaries make you physically and emotionally vulnerable and can lead to dangerous situations.

Unfortunately, some people have a problem knowing what "normal" is. In Teresa's story, Sam was a good example of someone who comes from a family that doesn't provide good role models. He saw the way his father physically and verbally hurt his mother, causing the emotional compass of the entire family to be jarred. Relationships with others became "all-or-nothing" affairs. If Teresa wouldn't share intimate thoughts and feelings with him, then he wouldn't be her friend at all.

Sam was a sexual groomer. (See page 49 for an explanation of what a "groomer" is.) He learned that from his dad. He should not be trusted. He needs to change, and only competent adults can help him do that.

Unhealthy
BOUNDARIES

Rigid Boundaries

Boundaries can be too rigid. Yes, having boundaries that are too rigid can be unhealthy. Here are some characteristics of unhealthy boundaries:

- Not allowing anyone to get close

- Never talking about personal feelings, wants, or needs

- Never sharing your emotions with your parents or brothers or sisters

- Having difficulty choosing and keeping friends

- Avoiding relationships outside your family by isolating yourself from classmates and acquaintances

Loose Boundaries

Boundaries can also be too loose or weak. These types of boundary situations usually lead to hurt and a lowered self-worth:

- Displaying inappropriate affection

- Always doing what others say; never disagreeing or saying "no"

- Saying or doing sexually suggestive things in front of others

- Sharing too much personal information about yourself too soon

- Having many sexual experiences

- Being tricked into being abused and not seeking help

- Doing anything to avoid conflict

- Taking responsibility for others' feelings

Do any of these characteristics describe your boundaries? Which ones?

If you have a boundary that is too loose or too rigid, explain what you do and why you do it.

Boundary Violations

How can people violate your boundaries? These behaviors are examples of boundary violations:

- Interrupting your conversations

- Taking your possessions

- Teasing that hurts you

- Asking personal questions that are inappropriate

- Gossiping about you

- Always hanging around you, invading your "private space"

- Saying or doing things that are offensive or vulgar

- Always trying to sit or stand too close to you

- Forcing you to do something sexual

- Physically or sexually abusing you

- Using inappropriate language or touch

Suppose you had a friend who was always sitting too close to you and it made you feel uncomfortable. How could you tell your friend that it made you feel uncomfortable?

What should you do if your friend did not move but instead made excuses?

If you knew someone who seemed lonely and isolated, what would you do or say to make friends with him or her?

Describe what you think your boundaries are. List what is okay to put up with and what is not.

If you are putting up with some things that are not okay, how do you plan to change them?

GROOMING

What Is Grooming?

When a person, whether male or female, plays with someone's feelings in order to gain control of the other person, that process is called "grooming." The groomer wants to prepare that person for some type of behavior.

If you don't have the experience or knowledge to recognize the tactics of an emotional groomer, you can be talked into doing something wrong without knowing it. You need to remember that the groomer is very skilled at manipulation and persuasion. Even when you begin to feel that something is wrong, the groomer can skillfully find ways to get what he or she wants.

Think of the story about the spider and fly: The spider was sneaky and tried to convince the fly to come into his web. He lured the fly by promising all kinds of good things. Then, when the fly believed the promises and went into the web, it was too late. The fly was trapped, and the spider was in control.

Groomers want to control their victims as the spider did. They will use your emotions and common sense against you.

And remember that the spider was charming, friendly, and fun to be with – until it was too late. Groomers behave the same way.

Grooming Tactics

Some groomers use the following tactics to manipulate you into doing something that is harmful.

- Jealousy and Possessiveness

- Insecurity

- Anger

- Intimidation

- Accusations

- Flattery

- Status

- Bribery

- Control

On the following pages you will see examples of how these tactics may be used to play on your emotions.

Jealousy and Possessiveness

Groomers feel they completely own your feelings and behaviors and are resentful and extremely jealous of anyone who gets attention from their "possessions." Because they don't want to share your attention, groomers want to remove other people and relationships from your life. This may mean they don't even want you to talk with other people.

"I'm telling you now and one time only, I want his stuff out of your locker. I don't care if you say he is just a good friend. What kind of fool do I look like? If you're my girl, his stuff has to go. If you want him, it can stay. Your choice!"

Has someone been extremely jealous of you or someone you care about? How did you react?

Insecurity

Groomers can act insecure and ask for constant reassurance of your loyalty to them. You are expected to take care of their insecurity. This works well with "people pleasers."

"I guess it's no big deal. I just think I'm not good enough for you. I'm not worth it. So let me know if you want to stop our relationship."

Or, the groomer may play on your insecurities or try to create new insecurities.

"No one else will ever want you. I'm the only one who is ever going to want you. You'd be stupid to pass up someone like me."

Has anyone tried to make you feel insecure in order to get you to do something you didn't want to?

_____

_____

_____

_____

_____

_____

_____

How did you handle it?

_____

_____

_____

_____

_____

_____

_____

_____

_____

Anger

Anger is a way for the groomer to control you or get what he or she wants. The groomer frequently is angry about something and may argue violently with you.

Emotional groomers who use anger can be very dangerous. Over time, their outbursts may happen more frequently or become more violent. They sometimes connect sex with the power their anger has given them.

"So he called you? What was his name? I know you at least know that. I've told you not to mess with me! People get hurt when they mess with me. If I find out you are, be ready, because I'm going to…"

Can you think of a time when someone used anger toward you? How did you react?

What was the outcome?

Intimidation

Intimidation is another powerful way groomers control others. Groomers are skilled at intimidating others with just a look or a word; glaring or staring can be used to scare or intimidate. They might threaten to hurt you or someone you like. These scare tactics usually work, and you become afraid to say "no." Girls may aim their hostility at other girls who threaten their relationships.

"I'm not mad at you, as long as you're not lying to me. If I find out you are lying, you and me are finished. So if you're not telling me something, you better spill it now. I don't want to have to find out later from someone else."

"I could slash her tires so easy. She'd better know who she's dealing with if she goes after you."

Physical actions can also be intimidating – standing over someone while he or she is seated, standing too close, touching, grabbing, using a loud voice or language. Guys can take intimidating stances when girls walk by – holding their crotches, making obscene signals with their hands, wagging their tongues, or making other gestures that could indicate that they are "nobody to mess with."

Has someone ever tried to intimidate you? What did you do?

Could you have handled it better? How?

Accusations

Emotional groomers may accuse you of doing all sorts of things that you didn't do. They could say that you were flirting with someone else or that you were talking behind their backs. Accusations also can indicate that the groomer is insecure and needs to be assured that he or she is "the only one."

"You just happened to walk into class with her. I saw you walking the halls with her. How dumb do you think I am?"

"Just tell me or not if you did anything with him. If you want him, just go out with him. I'll get over it. It's not like you would really care anyway. Don't do this to me; even when I hear this stuff, it hurts my feelings. I wouldn't be surprised if you're playing on me. I should have known better."

Has someone ever accused you of doing something you didn't do? How did you react? What happened?

Flattery

Most emotional groomers are "smooth talkers." They know what to say to impress others and appear completely trustworthy. They use language cons that lure the victim into thinking he or she is the most important person in the world. Groomers do not give sincere or honest compliments. They use exaggerated and insincere comments to get what they want.

We all like to hear nice things about us, but it's important to know the difference between praise and flattery. Praise means showing approval or admiration for people. It is specific and truthful. Flattery is phony and overdone and usually is used to get something from someone.

"If I told you you had a really gorgeous body, would you hold it against me?"

"You look really hot today, baby!"

"There's a lot of things I love about you. You're the smartest, sweetest, most handsome guy in…"

Give an example of a compliment you have received that you thought was sincere:

_____

_____

_____

_____

_____

_____

_____

_____

Have you ever received flattery that sounded phony or overdone? What was it?

_____

_____

_____

_____

_____

_____

_____

_____

_____

Status

Sometimes others "look up" to groomers. They could be good athletes, have a lot of money or designer clothes, have access to alcohol or drugs, or have a tough or glamorous reputation. They use their popularity and status to lure you to and keep you in a sexual relationship. Having sex also can be a way to gain status. In some gangs, part of the initiation involves a sexual conquest.

"I do like you a lot even though we're not going out. If I didn't would I waste five minutes of a phone call on you? Would I call you when there's a lot more girls that I could be calling? I'm not too good for you at all because there's no such thing. Please believe me, I do care and like you and I wouldn't be wasting my time if I didn't."

Can you think of some examples where friends or classmates have used their popularity, money, or other status symbols to manipulate others?

Bribery

Giving gifts can be a normal sign of friendship or love, but groomers give gifts to charm you into pleasing them. Victims may feel that they need to "pay back" the groomers. Sometimes the promise of marriage or always being together is used to convince victims to stay with groomers. Bribery can be very blatant. Many young males feel that spending money on girls means that they should expect sex in return.

"If I could do it I'd buy you everything you wanted. Remember that sweater in the mall. That would look so good on you baby. Someday I'll buy it or steal it if I have to."

How would you turn down a gift from someone you knew was using the gift to get you to do something that was wrong?

Control

Groomers want to control how you think and feel. They hold power over you any way they can. They will use some or all of the tactics we've listed, but their aim is to gain and keep control of you. In fact, most groomers will use a combination of these tactics to get what they want. If one tactic doesn't work, they will try another until one works. No matter how long it takes, the groomer finds a way to make you feel completely helpless and powerless to do anything about it.

List three different ways in
which others have inappropriately
controlled you. How did they make
you feel?

1. _____

_____

_____

_____

_____

_____

2. _____

_____

_____

_____

_____

3. _____

_____

_____

_____

_____

Have you been used by a groomer?

What tactics did the groomer use?

What did you do?

_____
_____
_____
_____
_____
_____
_____
_____

Would you handle it differently now?

_____
_____
_____
_____
_____
_____
_____
_____
_____

RELATIONSHIPS

How We Are Connected

We all start off life with built-in relationships. We all are connected to someone who takes care of us: parents, grandparents, relatives, foster parents, or other caring people. These people are closest to us in our boundary wheel

- at the beginning of life.

- at the center of our life.

Sometimes, though we are not so lucky. The parent or relative who was there at the beginning may not be available when we most need them. Dad may be gone and outside our boundary wheel altogether. Mom may be at the center of our wheel, but she may be ill. We may even have strained relationships with brothers and sisters. If Mom and Dad aren't there, we need to turn to other significant adults in our life who care for us very much.

Relationships with classmates, neighbors, and co-workers can be wonderful. But, like anything else in life, some relationships don't quite work out as we would like. Not all relationships are healthy and good for us.

Sometimes it's hard to figure out who is good for us and who isn't. Some classmates or co-workers play games, take advantage of us, or just take something from us. Some use force, manipulation, or our emotions to get what they want from us. If your boundaries are not where they should be, you could get hurt.

Trina's Story

Trina was thrilled when her classmate Mike first asked her out. He was cute and popular and was well liked by most of the kids in school. Trina and Mike seemed like the perfect couple. The other girls envied her, and she liked that.

They hadn't been dating long when Mike first said he was falling in love with her. He was attentive, drove her to school, ate lunch with her, called her. She loved it. She had finally found a guy who listened and who enjoyed being with her. Her whole life was revolving around someone who really cared for her. Then it happened. After a party, Mike got upset with her, grabbed her arm, and shouted at her. After a while he said, "Trina, look, I'm sorry I yelled at you. Let's forget it, okay? I'll call you tomorrow." She felt better that he had apologized to her.

But that was just the beginning. Mike became more and more controlling. He wanted to be with Trina all the time. His attentiveness started feeling more like possessiveness. He was very jealous and didn't want her talking with other guys.

"It won't happen again." She had heard those words often since the first time he grabbed her arm. She couldn't count the number of times he had slapped, grabbed, shaken, or yelled at her. He was always sorry after it happened and bought her gifts to prove how much he cared.

Abusive Relationships

Trina's story is like those of thousands of teenagers who have fallen into an abusive dating relationship. Most people don't want to admit they are in a harmful relationship. They want to believe that everything is okay, but they don't see the truth.

Many people avoid the pain of a breakup by thinking that things will work out. It often seems too difficult to sort through the maze of emotions surrounding the relationship. The truth is, relationships can flourish, get boring, grow sour, or even become abusive. People have to work at getting along with others; there are no quick and easy ways, no shortcuts to healthy relationships.

Have you or someone you know ever been in an abusive relationship?

How was it abusive?

What's the relationship like today?

Danger Signs

If you are in a relationship in which any of the following is taking place, the chances of having a positive relationship are slim. Get out of the relationship.

One-Sidedness

One person dominates the relationship. You have to constantly give in.

Manipulation

The person does anything to get what he or she wants. You feel manipulated.

Possessiveness

The person becomes extremely jealous if you talk to or hang around other people. You feel that you can't be yourself.

Unrealistic Demands

The person tells you that you must think, act, or dress a certain way. You have to always do what the other person wants instead of compromising or taking turns.

Anger

The person gets extremely angry or violent. You are hurt and afraid or think it's your fault.

Build Healthy Relationships

Learn to recognize people who don't have your best interests at heart so you can avoid them. And learn to recognize those who do have your best interests at heart. Learn to recognize the qualities that make a good relationship, and work on keeping relationships healthy.

Take your time.

Really getting to know and trust someone occurs as you have many experiences together.

Balance the give and take.

Make sure there is a healthy balance of give and take. Neither person should control the relationship.

Don't worry too much.

Don't allow yourself to spend a great deal of time worrying about your relationship.

Adjust to change.

Realize that relationships constantly change, and learn how to adjust to these changes. You may drift away from a close friend if your interests change. Or you could decide to start dating someone as your friendship grows closer.

Examine past relationships.

Look at past relationships, and use what you learned to make a current one better.

Look for good qualities.

Write down why certain people make good friends, and look for those qualities when seeking new friends. Steer clear of people who don't have those qualities.

Do you ever feel used or treated like an object at school, at work, or in a friendship? Explain.

Have you ever been threatened
with words or force? Explain.

How often do you think about a particular relationship? Does this take time away from other responsibilities? Explain.

How can you start building healthier relationships?

FRIENDSHIPS

What a Friend Should Be

Friends are special people because you do things *for* them as well as *with* them. Friends are there for the good times, bad times, and all the times in between.

When we mention the word "friend," many things come to mind – fondness, sharing, hanging out together. Having friends is a way of knowing that life is more fun.

The first task of a girl is to learn how to be a friend to other girls. The first task of a boy is to learn how to be a friend to other boys. All genuine friendships have the characteristics described on the following pages.

Friends share.

- They have common interests.

- They share happy times.

- They comfort each other in sad times.

- They share fears and secrets without being afraid that a friend will tell others.

Friends like each other.

- You give a lot.

- You receive a lot.

- Friendship ends when you or your friend quits giving.

Friendships are not exclusive.

- You both have other friends.

- You are not considered each other's "property."

Friends trust each other.

- A friend is reliable.

- A friend is committed.

- A friend doesn't manipulate.

- A friend wouldn't try to talk you into doing something illegal or immoral.

- A friend won't abandon you.

Friends help each other get better.

- Friends talk you out of destructive behavior.

- Friends tell you what you need to hear and not just what you want to hear.

Friendship is different from companionship.

- Friends are not people you just do things *with*, but people you do things *for*.

- There is more caring between friends than between companions.

Examples of Unhealthy Friendships

Following are some examples of friendships in which the "friends" are not equals. One friend is taking advantage of the other in the relationship.

The Intimidator

The intimidator usually demands or assumes that his or her needs will be met, and the other person gives in just to keep the friendship going, even though he or she may feel controlled and resentful. This is not a true friendship.

Gina was in her dorm room dressing for class. After wasting 10 minutes searching for the shirt she'd planned to wear, she had to rush to class at the last minute. There sat her roommate, Becky, wearing the shirt she'd been looking for. "All my clothes were dirty," Becky said. "I borrowed it while you were in the shower. I knew you wouldn't mind."

How do you attempt to set limits in a relationship like this one? If you have an intimidator for a friend, you need to confront him or her, setting limits to protect yourself from further hurt. Then the two of you can re-negotiate the relationship by setting new ground rules.

The 'Can't Say No' Buddy

This person finds it difficult to say "no" within a friendship. In order to avoid all conflict, he or she avoids speaking plainly and is just too nice.

Thad asks Keisha, "Marcie's having a party Saturday night. She says her parents won't be home. I hear it'll be wild. Want to go?" Keisha answers, "I guess I'll go if you want to." Keisha doesn't tell Thad that she's uncomfortable about going to the party because she knows she'll have to lie to her parents in order to go. But she's afraid that by speaking up she'll jeopardize her friendship with Thad.

Honesty is one of the most important facets of friendship. How could Keisha tell Thad her true feelings about the party without hurting their friendship? Do you ever have trouble telling a friend exactly how you feel about something?

The User

Do you have "friends" who often call on you for help in self-caused emergencies? Many "friendships" can get caught in this type of interaction.

"Jake, I'm late for work, and I don't have enough gas in my car to make it. Can I borrow your car?"

Jake's "friend" is manipulating him, using Jake to get out of a jam he created by not thinking ahead.

If you have so-called friends like this, you need to tell them you feel used and taken advantage of. They are probably aware of how they are hurting you but may not want to admit it, even to themselves. They are just plain selfish. Let them know that you won't be able to help out in their "emergencies" anymore. This makes them more accountable for themselves, and the friendship, if it is a real friendship, will grow stronger over time.

The Coaster

In some relationships, one person does all the work, takes all the initiative, and makes all the plans, while the other person "coasts," putting no effort into maintaining the friendship.

"Sorry, Jamie, but I can't go to the game with you this Friday. Why don't you give me a call next weekend, and maybe we can do something then."

Instead of offering to set up the plans for the following weekend, Jamie's "friend" is just coasting along. In a relationship like this, the person doing all the work is likely to feel resentful and frustrated; the other wonders what the problem is. Is this what friendship is all about?

In friendships, both parties need to take responsibility for the relationship. You need to set limits with your "friends," letting each carry his or her own weight. You may find out that a friendship isn't mutual, and you can move on to another one. Or you may use this chance to work on building a better, more solid relationship.

Do you currently have friendships that are not equal or are in conflict? If so, what new skills can you use to equalize the friendship or resolve the conflict?

If you could visualize "friendship" as a piece of art, what would it look like?

RELATIONSHIPS

& Your Future

Good Friendships

To *have* a good friend you must also *be* a good friend. Good friendships need equal give and take, understanding, and patience. How to nourish the good friendships you have:

- Permit your friends to be themselves.

- Give each other space.

- Be ready to give and to receive.

- Make your advice constructive.

- Be loyal.

- Give praise and encouragement.

- Be honest.

- Treat friends as equals.

- Be someone your friends can trust.

- Be willing to risk vulnerability.

Bad Friendships

Sometimes we end up in bad friendships. We may feel that something is wrong, but we just don't know what it is. The actions and words of our so-called friend are inappropriate and make us feel uncomfortable.

Here are some signs that you may be in a bad friendship:

- You can't be yourself without getting criticism from your "friend."

- Your "friend" doesn't give you any space.

- Your "friend" is pushy, wanting everything his or her way.

- Your "friend" is overly critical of you and others.

- Your "friend" is jealous of you and other friends.

- Your "friend" may lie to you, teachers, or parents.

- You feel that your "friend" directs "put-downs" toward you and others.

- Your "friend" does not treat you as an equal.

Sometimes "friends" will say things to you that make you feel uncomfortable. People who say these things are not true friends. Here are some examples of how they may violate your boundaries:

"Hey, let's skip math today and go to the mall."

"You know, if you loved me, you'd have sex with me."

"You watch the door while I steal the answer key for the next test."

"I have a hard time sitting next to you and not touching you; hope you don't mind if I just rub your leg while we sit here?"

When people have healthy boundaries, conversations tend to be more positive. You feel more comfortable around these people.

"Did you know that Cara is sick? How about if we stop by and say 'Hi' before we head home?"

"Marcus keeps asking me to smoke pot with him, and it makes me uncomfortable. I think I'm just going to tell him I'm not interested in hanging with someone who uses dope. If he decides to quit, I'd like to hang with him again."

"I don't agree with you on that, but I do respect your feelings."

Solving Relationship Problems

So, are you now ready to go out and set new boundaries? It will take time and practice to learn when to say "no" or "yes" to people, but the right answer will help you take control of your life. The steps you take should be small, and the success you see will grow with each step you take.

When you are trying to solve a personal problem, it helps to write down your thoughts as you are working it out.

My problem is:

_____

_____

_____

_____

_____

_____

_____

_____

_____

_____

I am feeling:

My goal is:

Some possible solutions are:

a.

b.

c.

What might happen if I choose each of these solutions?

a.

b.

c.

My plan for solving my problem is:

_____

_____

_____

_____

_____

_____

_____

_____

_____

_____

_____

_____

_____

_____

_____

_____

_____

_____

_____

_____

_____

_____

_____

_____

After I tried my solution, I found
that it worked:
❑ very well
❑ okay
❑ not so well
❑ terribly

The next time something like this
happens, I might try:

Getting Started

The bottom line is this: We want real friends. Real friends do not violate our boundaries. They do not talk us into things we should not be doing. They help us be moral, upright people. Real friends help us maintain our foundational values and have good relationships with our parents, our brothers and sisters, friends and acquaintances.

Start by setting healthy boundaries, and surround yourself with people who respect them. When you stick with the rules you have set, you will protect yourself and will likely find people who are good for you. Then in return you can be a good friend to them also. True friendship is not necessarily an easy road, but it's well worth the travel.

Good luck in your journey to newer, healthier boundaries and better friendships.

Additional Reading for Teens

A Good Friend: How to Make One, How to Be One
Ron Herron & Val J. Peter
Boys Town Press
Father Flanagan's Boys' Home
Boys Town, NE 68010

Who's in the Mirror? Finding the Real Me
Ron Herron & Val J. Peter
Boys Town Press
Father Flanagan's Boys' Home
Boys Town, NE 68010

*What's Right for Me? Making Good
Choices in Relationships*
Ron Herron & Val J. Peter
Boys Town Press
Father Flanagan's Boys' Home
Boys Town, NE 68010

**For a free Boys Town Press catalog,
call 1-800-282-6657 or visit
boystownpress.org**